THE JAPJI AND THE REHRAS
The Morning and Evening Prayers of the Sikhs

THE JAPJI
and
THE REHRAS

The Morning and Evening Prayers of the Sikhs

translated by

KHUSHWANT SINGH

illustrated by

Mohit Suneja

RAINLIGHT
RUPA

Published in RAINLIGHT by
Rupa Publications India Pvt. Ltd 2013
7/16, Ansari Road, Daryaganj
New Delhi 110002

Sales centres:
Allahabad Bengaluru Chennai
Hyderabad Jaipur Kathmandu
Kolkata Mumbai

Text Copyright © Khushwant Singh 2013
Illustration Copyright © Rupa Publications India Pvt. Ltd 2013

ISBN: 978-81-291-2409-8

10 9 8 7 6 5 4 3 2 1

The moral right of the author has been asserted.

Printed at Lustra Print Process Pvt. Ltd.

To Dr Prabha Manchanda—
in gratitude for her caring and concern

ਸਤਿਨਾਮੁ
ਕਰਤਾ ਪੁਰਖੁ
ਨਿਰਭਉ ਨਿਰਵੈਰੁ
ਅਕਾਲ ਮੂਰਤਿ ਅਜੂਨਿ
ਸੈਭੰ ਗੁਰਪ੍ਰਸਾਦਿ

introduction

I am not a religious man, but I call myself a Sikh and am proud to be one. As with every religion, Sikhism has been misinterpreted by bigoted and cynical people, but that is a failure of men, not of the faith. In its essence, Sikhism remains a great religion that teaches all that I value: tolerance, simplicity, equality, service to the community and to all humanity.

Sikhism was born of and influenced by the two dominant faiths of Punjab, Hinduism and Islam. Guru Nanak (1469-1539)—the founder of the Sikh religion—drew upon Hindu Bhakta and Islamic Sufi philosophy to spread a message of love and universal brotherhood, and of simple worship beyond dogma and empty ritual. His teachings fired the imagination of the peasants of Punjab, and he became the beloved saint of both Hindus and Muslims. Even today, he is remembered as the king of holy men:

Baba Nanak shah fakir
Hindu ka guru musalman ka pir

(Baba Nanak, the King of Fakirs,
To the Hindu a Guru, to the Muslim a Pir)

Nanak was followed by nine Gurus, who carried forward his legacy and consolidated the Sikh faith.

Sikhism preaches belief in the unity of God (*Ek Omkar:* God is One) and equates God with truth (*Sat Naam:* His Name is Truth). Sikhs do not believe in sacred rivers or mountains, nor do they worship idols: 'To be saved, worship only the Truth,' said Nanak. The Sikhs do not have priests. There are, now, professional scripture readers (granthis) and musicians (ragis), but in fact, irrespective of status, all Sikhs are competent to perform religious ceremonies.

The Sikh religion does not recognize the caste system. Nanak's teachings and verses abound with passages that describe as ungodly the conduct of those who treat anyone as untouchable. Among the first five Sikhs to be chosen as the Khalsa (the Pure) by the last Sikh Guru, Gobind Singh, was a Dalit, Bhai Dharam Singh. (Unfortunately, many Sikhs still discriminate against the lower castes, and fail their faith and their Gurus.)

A feature of the Sikh religion which is particularly striking is its emphasis on prayer. The form of prayer is usually the repetition of the name of God and chanting hymns of praise. Sacred hymns composed by the first five Gurus and the ninth Guru, and by Bhakti and Sufi saints like Kabir, Baba Farid and Mira Bai, were compiled and collected in the Adi Granth, or Granth Sahib, the holy book of the Sikhs, by Arjun Dev (the fifth Guru) and Gobind Singh (the tenth and last Guru). The hymns of the Adi Granth are divided into thirty-one ragas, in which they are meant to be sung. The Gurus believed that repeating the name of God and divine worship through music were the best means of attaining the state of bliss—vismad—that resulted in communion with the Almighty.

When Gobind Singh declared that with him the line of succession of the Sikh Gurus had ended, he asked his followers to look upon the Adi Granth as the symbolic representation of all the ten Gurus. Since then, it has been the central object of Sikh worship and ritual.

The Japji—the morning prayer—was composed by the first Guru, Nanak, himself, and appears at the very beginning of the Adi Granth. It consists of the mool mantra—the root or primal mantra—that is the basis of Sikh theology, followed by thirty-eight pauris, or hymns, and a final shloka. All of it does not seem to have been written at one time and the length of its verses, their metre and thought content varies. The verses are in the nature of meditations, dealing with the fundamentals of the Sikh faith. In these verses, Nanak mentions four successive steps towards salvation: dharam khand, gyan khand, karam khand and sach khand, corresponding to discipline, knowledge, action, and ending with the blissful merger with God. These steps follow very closely the four stages of the spiritual progress of the Sufis.

Unlike the rest of the Granth Sahib, the Japji was not set to music and is never sung. The language of the Japji is the Punjabi of the fifteenth century and is extremely difficult to translate. My translation is largely based on the commentaries of the famous Punjabi poet and scholar Bhai Vir Singh.

The Rehras is the evening prayer, recited around sunset. It comprises verses by five Gurus—Nanak, Amar Das, Ram Das, Arjun Dev and Gobind Singh. The origin of the word 'rehras' is disputed by scholars and theologians. The most widely accepted interpretation is that it stands for 'humble invocation'.

The Rehras as a prayer is not mentioned as such in the Adi Granth, and it has been used only once as a word—*Har kirat hamri Rehras* ('That I sing God's praises is my humble invocation')—in the main body of the prayer. But there is reason to believe that the Rehras, in some form or the other, has been recited at close of day since the time of Guru Nanak. Bhai Gurdas, who was a near contemporary of Guru Nanak and lived up to the time of Guru Arjun, records:

Saajhey Sodar gaaviye
Man maele kar mael milandey.

(The like-minded met, and together
They chanted Sodar in the evening.)

And the fact that the Rehras was being referred to as a complete prayer during Guru Gobind Singh's time is evident from Bhai Nand Lal's *Bin Rehras sama jo khovey* ('Whosoever wastes time without reciting the Rehras...')

The Rehras does indeed begin with Guru Nanak's 'Sodar'—the doorway to God's mansion. This is repeated from the Japji, but with a change in tone and a few of the words changed—mainly because the Japji is in the nature of an instruction from God, while the Rehras is the devotee's hymn of gratitude to God. Compositions of other gurus were added to the original Sodar in later years. The quatrains of Gobind Singh were the last to be incorporated.

The content of the Rehras can be divided into three broad strands—the quest, the striving and the culmination. This last is expressed in a verse by the third Guru, Amar Das:

Anand bhaiya meri maae
Sat guru main paaya.

(O mother I have attained bliss,
I have found the true Guru I was searching for.)

The Japji and the Rehras are two of the most popular and sacred prayers of the Sikhs. I hope these translations will communicate some of the power and poignancy of the verses to people unable to read the originals in Gurmukhi.

—*Khushwant Singh*

THE JAPJI

The Morning Prayer of the Sikhs

There is One God.

He is the Supreme Truth.

He, the Creator,

Is without fear and without hate.

He, the Omnipresent,

Pervades the universe.

He is not born,

Nor does He die to be born again.

By His grace shalt thou worship Him.

Before time itself

There was truth.

When time began to run its course

He was the truth.

Even now, He is the truth

And evermore shall truth prevail.

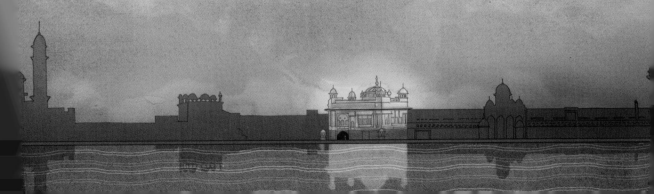

1

Not by thought alone can He be known,
Though one think a hundred thousand times;
Not in solemn silence
Nor in deep meditation.
Though fasting yields
an abundance of virtue
It cannot appease the hunger for truth.
No, by none of these,
Nor by a hundred thousand other devices,
Can God be reached.
How then shall the truth be known?
How the veil of false illusion torn?
O Nanak, thus runneth the writ divine,
The righteous path—let it be thine.

2

By Him are all forms created,
By Him infused with life and blessed,
By Him are some to excellence elated,
Others born lowly and depressed.
By His writ some have pleasure,
    others pain;
By His grace some are saved,

Others doomed to die, re-live, and die again.

His will encompasseth all, there be none beside.

O Nanak, He who knows, hath no ego and no pride.

3

Who has the power to praise His might?

Who has the measure of His bounty?

Of His portents who has the sight?

Who can value His virtue, His deeds, His charity?

Who has the knowledge of His wisdom,

Of His deep, impenetrable thought?

How worship Him who creates life, then destroys,

And having destroyed doth re-create?

How worship Him who appeareth far

Yet is ever present and proximate?

There is no end to His description,

Though the speakers and their speeches be legion.

He the Giver ever giveth,

We who receive grow weary,

On His bounty humanity liveth

Form primal age to posterity.

4

God is the Master, God is truth,

His name spelleth love divine,

His creatures ever cry: 'O give, O give,'

He the bounteous doth never decline.

What then in offering shall we bring

That we may see his court above?

What then shall we say in speech

That hearing may evoke His love?

In the ambrosial hours of fragrant dawn

On truth and greatness ponder in meditation,

Though action determine how thou be born,

Through grace alone comes salvation.

O Nanak, this need we know alone,

That God and truth are two in one.

5

He cannot be proved, for He is uncreated;

He is without matter, self-existent.

They that serve shall honoured be,

O Nanak, the Lord is most excellent.

Praise the Lord, hear them that do Him praise,

In your hearts His name be graven,

Sorrows from your soul erase
And make your hearts a joyous haven.

The Guru's word has the sage's wisdom,
The Guru's word is full of learning,
For though it be the Guru's word
God Himself speaks therein.

Thus run the words of the Guru:
'God is the destroyer, preserver and creator,
God is the Goddess too.
Words to describe are hard to find,
I would venture if I knew.'
This alone my teacher taught,
There is but one Lord of all creation,
Forget Him not.

6

If it please the Lord, in holy waters would I bathe,
If it please Him not, worthless is that pilgrimage.

This is the law of all creation,
That nothing's gained save by action.
Thy mind, wherein buried lie,

Precious stones, jewels, gems,

Shall opened be if thou but try

And hearken to the Guru's word.

This the Guru my teacher taught,

There is but one Lord of all creation,

Forget Him not.

7

Were life's span extended to the four ages
    and ten times more,

Were one known over the nine continents

Ever in humanity's fore,

Were one to achieve greatness

With a name noised over the earth,

If one found not favour with the Lord

What would it all be worth?

Among the worms be as vermin,

By sinners be accused of sin.

O Nanak, the Lord fills the vicious with virtue,

The virtuous maketh more true.

Knowest thou of any other

Who in turn could the Lord thus favour?

8

By hearing the word, men achieve wisdom,
    saintliness, courage and contentment.

By hearing the word, men learn of the earth,
    the power that supports it and the firmament.

By hearing the word, men learn of the upper
    and nether regions, of islands and continents.

By hearing the word, men conquer the fear of death
    and the elements.

O Nanak, the word hath such magic for the worshippers,
Those that hear, death do not fear,
Their sorrows end and sins disappear.

9

By hearing the word
Mortals are to godliness raised.
By hearing the word,
The foul-mouthed are filled with pious praise.
By hearing the word,
Are revealed the secrets of the body and of nature.

By hearing the word,

Is acquired the wisdom of all the scriptures.

O Nanak, the word hath such magic for the worshippers,

Those that hear, death do not fear,

Their sorrows end and sins disappear.

10

By hearing the word, one learns of truth,

    contentment, and is wise.

By hearing the word, the need for pilgrimages does not arise.

By hearing the word, the student achieves

    scholastic distinction.

By hearing the word, the mind

is easily led to meditation.

O Nanak, the word hath such

magic for the worshippers,

Those that hear, death

do not fear,

Their sorrows end and

sins disappear.

11

By hearing the word, one sounds the depths of virtue's sea.

By hearing the word, one acquires learning, holiness and royalty.

By hearing the word, the blind see and their paths are visible.

By hearing the word, the fathomless becomes fordable.

O Nanak, the word hath such magic for the worshippers,

Those that hear, death do not fear,

Their sorrows end and sins disappear.

12

The believer's bliss one cannot describe,

He who endeavours regrets in the end,

There is no paper, pen, nor any scribe

Who can the believer's state comprehend.

The name of the Lord is immaculate.

He who would know must have faith.

13

The believer hath wisdom and understanding;
The believer hath knowledge of all the spheres;
The believer shall not stumble in ignorance,
Nor of death have any fears.

The name of the Lord is immaculate,
He who would know must have faith.

14

The believer's way is of obstructions free;
The believer is honoured in the presence sublime;
The believer's path is not lost in futility,
For faith hath taught him law divine.

The name of the Lord is immaculate,
He who would know must have faith.

15

The believer reaches the gate of salvation;
His kith and kin he also saves.
The believer beckons the congregation,
Their souls are saved from transmigration.
The name of the Lord is immaculate,
He who would know must have faith.

16

Thus are chosen the leaders of men,
Thus honoured in God's estimation:
Though they grace the courts of kings,
Their minds are fixed in holy meditation.
Their words are weighed with reason,
They know that God's works are legion.

Law which like the fabled bull supports the earth
Is of compassion born;
Though it bind the world in harmony,
Its strands are thin and worn.
He who the truth would learn,

Must know of the bull and the load it bore.

For there are worlds besides our own

And beyond them many more.

Who is it that bears these burdens?

What power bears him that beareth them?

Of creatures of diverse kinds and colours

The ever-flowing pen hath made record.

Can anyone write what it hath writ

Or say how great a task was it?

How describe His beauty and His might?

His bounty how estimate?

How speak of Him who with one word

Did the whole universe create,

And made a thousand rivers flow therein?

What might have I to praise Thy might?

I have not power to give it praise.

Whatever be Thy wish, I say Amen.

Mayst Thou endure, O Formless One.

17

There is no count of those who pray,

Nor of those who Thee adore;

There is no count of those who worship,

Nor of those who by penance set store.

There is no count of those who read the holy book aloud

Nor of those who think of the world's sorrows and lament.

There is no count of sages immersed in thought and reason,

Nor of those who love humanity and are benevolent.

There is no count of warriors who match their strength with steel,

Nor of those who contemplate in peace and are silent.

What might have I to praise Thy might?

I have not power to give it praise.

Whatever be Thy wish, I say Amen.

Mayst Thou endure, O Formless One.

18

There is no count of fools who will not see,

Nor of thieves who live by fraud,

There is no count of despots practising tyranny,

Nor of those whose hands are soiled with blood.

There is no count of those who sin and go free,

Nor of liars caught in the web of falsehood,

There is no count of the polluted who live on filth,

Nor of the evil-tongued weighed down with calumny.

Of such degradation, O Nanak, also think.

What might have I to praise Thy might?

I have not power to give it praise.

Whatever be Thy wish, I say Amen.

Mayst Thou endure, O Formless One.

19

Though there is no count of Thy names and habitations,

Nor of Thy regions uncomprehended,

Yet many there have been with reason perverted

Who to Thy knowledge have pretended.

Though by words alone we give Thee name and praise,

And by words, reason, worship and Thy virtue compute;

Though by words alone we write and speak

And by words our ties with Thee constitute;

The word does not its Creator bind,

What Thou ordainest we receive,

Thy creations magnify Thee,

Thy name in all places find.

What might have I to praise Thy might?

I have not power to give it praise.

Whatever be Thy wish, I say Amen.

Mayst Thou endure, O Formless One.

20

As hands or feet besmirched with slime,

Water washes white;

As garments dark with grime

Rinsed with soap are made light;

So when sin soils the soul

Prayer alone shall make it whole.

Words do not the saint or sinner make,

Action alone is written in the book of fate,

What we sow that alone we take;

O Nanak, be saved or forever transmigrate.

21

Pilgrimage, austerity, mercy,
almsgiving and charity
Bring merit, be it as little as the mustard seed;
But he who hears, believes and cherishes
the word,
An inner pilgrimage and cleansing is his meed.
All virtue is Thine, for I have none,
Virtue follows a good act done.
Blessed Thou the Creator, the Prayer, the Primal
Truth and beauty and longing eternal.
What was the time, what day of the week,
What the month, what season of the year,
When Thou didst create the earthly sphere?
The Pandit knows it not, nor is it writ in his Puran;
The Qadi knows it not, though he read
and copy the Koran.
The Yogi knows not the date nor the day of the week,
He knows not the month or even the season.
Only Thou who made it all can speak,
For knowledge is Thine alone.
How then shall I know Thee,
how describe, praise and name?
O Nanak, many there be who pretend
to know, each bolder in his claim.

All I say is: 'Great is the Lord, great His name;

What He ordains comes to be,'

O Nanak, he who sayeth more shall hereafter regret his stupidity.

─◦◦◦◦◦◦─

22

Numerous worlds there be in regions beyond the skies and below,

But the research-weary scholars say, we do not know.

The Hindu and the Muslim books are full of theories;

   the answer is but one.

If it could be writ, it would have been,

   but the writer thereof be none.

O Nanak, say but this, the Lord is great,

In His knowledge He is alone.

─◦◦◦◦◦◦─

23

Worshippers who praise the Lord

   know not His greatness,

As rivers and rivulets that flow into the sea know

   not its vastness.

Mighty kings with domains vaster than the ocean,

With wealth piled high in a mountainous heap

Are less than the little ant

That the Lord's name in its heart doth keep.

24

Infinite His goodness, and the ways of exaltation;

Infinite His creation and His benefaction;

Infinite the sights and sounds, infinite His great design;

Infinite its execution, infinite without confine.

Many there be that cried in pain to seek the end of all ending,

Their cries were all in vain, for the end is past understanding.

It is the end of which no one knoweth,

The more one says the more it groweth.

The Lord is of great eminence, exalted is His name.

He who would know His height, must in stature be the same.

He alone can His own greatness measure.

O Nanak, what He gives we must treasure.

25

Of His bounty one cannot write too much,

He the Great Giver desires not even a mustard seed;

Even the mighty beg at His door, and others such

Whose numbers can never be conceived.

There be those who receive but are self-indulgent,

Others who get but have no gratitude.

There be the foolish whose bellies are never filled,

Others whom hunger's pain doth ever torment.

All this comes to pass as Thou hast willed.

Thy will alone breaks mortal bonds,

No one else hath influence.

The fool who argues otherwise

Shall be smitten into silence.

The Lord knows our needs, and gives,

Few there be that count their blessings,

He who is granted gratitude and power to praise,

O Nanak, is the king of kings.

26

His goodness cannot be priced or traded,

Nor His worshippers valued, not their store;

Priceless too are dealers in the market sacred

With love and peace evermore.

Perfect His law and administration,

Precise His weights and measures;

Boundless His bounty and His omens,

Infinite mercy in His orders.

How priceless Thou art one cannot state,

Those who spoke are mute in adoration,

The readers of the scriptures expatiate,

Having read, are lost in learned conversation.

The great gods Brahma and Indra do Thee proclaim,

So do Krishna and his maidens fair;

Shiva and the Shaivites do Thee name;

The Buddhas Thou made, Thy name bear.

The demons and the demigods,

Men, brave men, seers and the sainted

Having discoursed and discussed

Have spoken and departed.

If Thou didst many more create

Not one could any more state,

For Thou art as great as is Thy pleasure,

O Nanak, Thou alone knowest Thy measure.

He who claims to know blasphemeth

And is the worst among the stupidest.

───◦◦◦───

27
sodar
(TE DEUM)

Where is the gate, where the mansion,

From whence Thou watchest all creation,

Where sounds of musical melodies,

Of instruments playing, minstrels singing,

Are joined in divine harmony?

There the breezes blow, the waters

    run and the fires burn,

There Dharmaraj, the King of

    Death, sits in state;

There the recording angels

    Chitra and Gupta write

For Dharmaraj to read and

    adjudicate.

There are the gods Ishwara

    and Brahma,

The goddess Devi of divine grace;

There Indra sits on his celestial throne

And lesser gods, each in his place.

There ascetics in deep meditation,

Holy men in contemplation,

The pure of heart, the continent,

Men of peace and contentment,

Doughty warriors never yielding,

Thy praises are ever singing.

From age, the pandit and the sage

Do Thee exalt in their study and their writing.

There maidens fair, heart bewitching,

Who inhabit the earth, the upper and the lower regions,

Thy praises chant in their singing.

By the gems that Thou didst create,

In the sixty-eight places of pilgrimage,

Is Thy name exalted.

By warriors strong and brave in strife,

By the sources four from whence came life,

Of egg or womb, of sweat or seed,

Is Thy name magnified.

The regions of the earth, the heavens and the universe

That Thou didst make and dost sustain,

Sing to Thee and praise Thy name.

Only those Thou lovest and with whom Thou art pleased

Can give Thee praise and in Thy love be steeped.

Others too there must be who Thee acclaim,

I have no memory of knowing them

Nor of knowledge, O Nanak, make a claim.

He alone is the Master True, Lord of the Word, ever the same,

He Who made creation is, shall be and shall ever remain;

He Who made things of diverse species, shapes and hues,

Beholds that His handiwork His greatness proves.

What He wills He ordains,

To Him no one can an order give,

For He, O Nanak, is the King of kings,

As He wills so we must live.

28

As a beggar goes a-begging,

Bowl in one hand, staff in the other,

Rings in his ears, in ashes smothered,

So go thou forth in life.

With earrings made of contentment,

With modesty thy begging bowl,

Meditation the fabric of thy garment,

Knowledge of death thy cowl,

Let thy mind be chaste, virginal clean,

Faith the staff on which to lean.

Thou shalt then thy fancy humiliate,

With mind subdued, the world subjugate.

Hail! And to Thee be salutation.

Thou art primal, Thou art pure,

Without beginning, without termination,

In single form, forever endure.

29

From the storehouse of compassion

Seek knowledge for thy food.

Let thy heartbeat be the call of the conch shell,

Blown in gratitude.

He is the Lord, His is the will, His the creation,

He is the Master of destiny, of union and separation.

Hail! And to Thee be salutation.

Thou art primal, Thou art pure,

Without beginning, without termination,

In single form, forever endure.

30

Maya, mythical goddess in wedlock divine,

Bore three gods accepted by all,

The creator of the world, the one who preserves,
And the one who adjudges its fall.
But it is God alone whose will prevails,
Others but their obedience render.
He sees and directs, but is by them unseen,
That of all is the greatest wonder.

Hail! And to Thee be salutation.
Thou art primal, Thou art pure,
Without beginning, without termination,
In single form, forever endure.

31

He hath His prayer-mat in every region,
In every realm His store.
To human beings He doth apportion
Their share for once and evermore.
The Maker having made doth His own creation view.
O Nanak, He made truth itself, for He Himself is true.

Hail! And to Thee be salutation.
Thou art primal, Thou art pure,
Without beginning, without termination,
In single form, forever endure.

32

Were I given a hundred thousand tongues instead of one
And the hundred thousand multiplied twenty-fold,
A hundred thousand times would I say, and say again,
The Lord of all the worlds is One.
That is the path that leads, these the steps that mount,
Ascend thus to the Lord's mansion
And with Him be joined in unison.
The sound of the songs of heaven thrills
The like of us who crawl, but desire to fly.
O Nanak, His grace alone it is that fulfils,
The rest mere prattle, and a lie.

33

Ye have no power to speak or in silence listen,
To grant or give away.
Ye have no power to live or die.
Ye have no power to acquire wealth and dominion,
To compel the mind to thought or reason,
To escape the world and fly.

He who hath the pride of power, let him try and see.
O Nanak, before the Lord there is no low or high degree.

34

He Who made the night and day,

The days of the week and the seasons,

He Who made the breezes blow, the waters run

The fires and the lower regions,

Made the earth—the temple of law.

He Who made creatures of diverse kinds

With a multitude of names,

Made this the law—

By thought and deed be judged forsooth,

For God is true and dispenseth truth.

There the elect His court adorn,

And God Himself their actions honours;

There are sorted deeds that were done and bore fruit

From those that to action could never ripen.

This, O Nanak, shall hereafter happen.

35

In the realm of justice there is law;

In the realm of knowledge there is reason.

Wherefore are the breezes, the waters and fire,

Gods that preserve and destroy, Krishnas and Shivas?

Wherefore are created forms, colours, attire,
Gods that create, the many Brahmas?

Here one strives to comprehend
The golden mount of knowledge ascend,
And learn as did the sage Dhruva.

Wherefore are the thunders and lightning,
The moons and suns, the world and its regions?
Wherefore are the sages, seers, wise men,
Goddesses, false prophets, demons and demigods,
Wherefore are there jewels in the ocean?
How many forms of life there be, how many tongues,
How many kings of proud ancestry?

Of these things many strive to know,
Many the slaves of reason.
Many there are,
O Nanak, their numbers are legion.

36

As in the realm of knowledge reason is triumphant,
And yields a myriad joys,
So in the realm of bliss is beauty resplendent.
There are fashioned forms of great loveliness;

Of them it is best to remain silent

Than hazard guesses and then repent.

There too are fashioned consciousness,

    understanding, mind and reason,

The genius of the sage and seer,

    the power of humans superhuman.

37

In the realm of action, effort is supreme,

Nothing else prevails.

There dwell doughty warriors brave and strong,

With hearts full of godliness,

And celestial maidens of great loveliness

Who sing their praise.

They cannot die nor be beguiled

For God Himself in their hearts resides.

There too are congregations of holy men

Who rejoice, for the Lord in their midst presides.

In the realm of truth is the Formless One

Who, having created, watches His creation

And graces us with the blessed vision.

There are the lands, the earths and the spheres

Of whose description there is not limit;

There by a myriad forms are a myriad purposes fulfilled,

What He ordains is in them instilled.

What He beholds, thinks and contemplates,

O Nanak, is too hard to state.

❦

38

If thou must make a gold coin true

Let thy mint these rules pursue.

In the forge of continence

Let the goldsmith be a man of patience,

His tools be made of knowledge,

His anvil made of reason;

With the fear of God the bellows blow,

With prayer and austerity make the fire glow,

Pour the liquid in the mould of love,

Print the name of the Lord thereon,

And cool it in the holy waters.

For thus in the mint of truth the word is coined,

Thus those who are graced are to work enjoined.

O Nanak, by his blessing have joy everlasting.

❦

shloka

Air, water and earth,

Of these are we made.

Air like the Guru's word gives the breath of life

To the babe born to the great mother earth

Sired by the waters.

The day and night our nurses be

That watch us in our infancy.

In their laps we play,

The world is our playground.

Our acts right and wrong at Thy court shall come to judgement;

Some be seated near Thy seat, some ever kept distant.

The toils have ended of those that have worshipped Thee,

O Nanak, their faces are lit with joyful radiance—

    many others they set free.

THE REHRAS

The Evening Prayer of the Sikhs

TRANSLATED BY
KHUSHWANT SINGH
WITH
REEMA ANAND

sodar

GURU NANAK

*Sodar—literally 'The Door'—is an eulogy to the creator of the universe,
the Sikh version of 'Te Deum' (to God). Lesser gods, goddesses, saints
and warriors and the elements join the chorus to sing praises of their creator.*

What kind of doorway? What kind of mansion?
Where You sit and care for Your creation!
Where melodies of countless strumming instruments,
And countless minstrels playing on it are heard.

In how many ragas and raginis are Your praises sung?
And how many celestial musicians sing of You?
'There'
Wind, water and fire glorify Your name,
'There'
Sings Dharmaraja
'There'
Sing Chitra and Gupta, the recording angels,
Putting up records for Dharmaraja to read and adjudicate

'There'

To Your glory sing,

Shiva, Brahma and goddesses adorned by You;

Indra on his celestial throne,

Together with other deities sings at Your door.

'There'

Ascetics in deep meditation

Holy men in contemplation

Long haired ascetics, men of truth

Men of peace and contentment

And warriors bold

Sing Your praises manifold.

Pandits through their scriptures,

Sages who have praised You from age to age;

Heart bewitching fairies in paradise,

Earth and regions underground

With Your praises resound.

Sparkling gems created by You,

And the sixty-eight places of pilgrimage with Your praise reverberate.

By doughty warriors brave in battle

By the sources four from where came life—

Of egg, womb, sweat or soil

Is Your name extolled and magnified

Countries, continents and worlds beyond this world which You
  made and sustained,
The entire cosmos sings praises to Your name.
Only those favoured by You
Can sing Your praises and get dyed in Your hue.
There must be Your other acclaimers of the same kind,
How far can Nanak stretch his mind?

It is He and eternally He alone who is our True Master
And truth is His name.
He is and ever will be, till eternity,
Never, will He fade,
The Creator of all infinity!

Creator of species in different colours and hues
Creator of Maya too;
Having created He watches over His creation
This His greatness proves.

What pleases Him, He ordains
None can order Him otherwise;
For He, O Nanak, is the King of kings
As He wills, so must we live.

sun vadda akhai sab koe

GURU NANAK

God's greatness is beyond assessing. It is only by His grace
that we can get a glimmer of how great He is.

> On hearing of Your greatness, all call You great.
> How great? Only one who has seen You can estimate!
> No one can assess Your worth, nor describe You
> All those who try get absorbed in You.

My great Master,

Of depth profound

An oceanful of virtues,

No one knows

The vastness of Your abound.

Even if all thinkers meet and contemplate about You,

All assessors together try to assess Your worth.

Theologians, meditators, gurus and great masters indeed,

Have not been able to grasp a jot of Your greatness.

All truths, all austerities, all goodness put together

Despite occult powers mustered by practitioners of the occult;

Without You none could attain perfection;

Whom You choose to grace,

Nothing can stand in his way.

What more can a poor devotee say?

Your treasury is full of grace

He whom You give,

Shall but give You praise,

Says Nanak, He alone perfects the truth and sustains.

aakhaan jeevan visrai mar jaon

Guru Nanak

People who forget to give thanks to the Lord who is their benefactor
are the lowest of the low.

Remembering You—I live
Distanced from You—I die.
It is very hard indeed
To meditate on the True Name.
If one hungers for the True Name
This hunger consumes all our pains.

Why then forget Him, mother mine?
True is our Master, true is His name.
So great is the worth of the True Name indeed,
Our praise is no more than a sesame seed.
We try and try and of trying tire,
Yet unable to assess His worth entire.
Joining hands to praise Him together,
Shall not magnify nor lessen His stature.

As He does not die

There is no reason to mourn,

He is ever-giving,

His bounty does not diminish.

He is the only one with this gift,

No one else possesses it.

There is none like Him

Nor ever will be.

Lord as mighty as You are, so is Your giving might

You gave us the day, then gave us the night.

Mean and lowly are they who forget the Lord

Says Nanak, without His name,

They are wretches outcaste.

har ke jan satgur satpurkha

GURU RAM DAS

Make singing hymns in praise of the Lord your daily evening prayer.
It is believed that the first two verses of this hymn were composed by Guru Ram Das
in answer to his father Guru Amar Das's request to spell out his wishes.
The remaining three verses deal with the importance of keeping company
with righteous men.

We seekers of the Lord beseech You our True Guru,

To You who is truth personified we pray;

We are but worms and vermin seeking Your protection,

Be merciful, illumine our hearts with Your name.

My Friend and Mentor, suffuse my heart with the name of Rama;

Let teachings of the Guru my life sustain

Let singing praises of the Lord show me the way

And be my evensong.

Men of the Lord are fortune's favourites

They are ever firm in their faith

And ever thirst for the Lord.

Finding the elixir of the Lord's name

Their thirsts are slaked.

In the company of holy men

His virtues they praise.

Most unfortunate are those,

And caught in shackles of life and death,

Who have not tasted the nectar of His name.

Those who sought not the Lord's protection

Nor the holy congregation,

Are damned in this life and for lives to come.

Those devotees blessed with the Guru's companionship,

Bear marks of blessed fate on their foreheads.

Twice blessed is that congregation

Where the nectar of the Lord's name is found.

There, says Nanak,

The Lord's name is illumined and enlightenment found.

kaahe re man chitve

GURU ARJAN DEV

When the Lord creates life, He provides sustenance for His creatures.
There is no need to burden one's mind with unnecessary worries.

> Why dear heart are you worried about what to do
> When the good Lord Himself provides sustenance for you.
> Creatures among rocks and boulders He created,
> Before them, their means of living He placed.
>
> Beloved Madhava! One who keeps company of saintly men is saved
> By Your grace, above others He is placed;

As out of dead wood,
Green leaves sprout.

Mother, father, kinsmen or wife
None will abide with you all your life!
The Lord provides for all mankind
Why then harbour fear within your mind?

As geese and swans fly hundred and hundreds of miles
Leaving their young behind!
Who feeds them? Who nurtures them?
They know and remember Him all the time.

All nine treasures and eighteen occult powers
Are in the palms of our Lord and Master,
For Him, will Nanak sacrifice his life over and over again.
There is no end to Your existence
Unmeasured forever will remain Your domain.

so purakh niranjan, hari purakh niranjan

GURU RAM DAS

He is immaculate and beyond comprehension.
There are many ways of worshipping Him.

Our Lord is without blemish, our Lord is untainted by illusion

He is beyond comprehension, endless and beyond reach;

All worship You, the real author of all creation;

All creatures are created by You, You are their provider and giver;

O men of God, ponder over Him! He is the remover of all sorrows;

He Himself the Lord, and the servant,

Says Nanak, of what worth is a mere human?

You dwell in every body, flowing uninterrupted,

You are the only one in every one;

Some You endow with riches, others You reduce to beggary,

It is all a part of Your inscrutable design;

You are the giver,

You Yourself the decider of how it is spent

I know not any other like You;

You are the infinite God, Your expanse unknown,

How can I put Your qualities in words?

Whoever serves You, on him will Nanak sacrifice his life.

Those who meditate on You, those who worship You,

Will live in peace for all their lives;

Those who meditate on You, will gain salvation

And be freed from the noose of Yama;

Those who worship the Lord who is without fear

They will themselves be freed of fear;

Those who serve the Lord

Will merge in the person of the Lord;

Twice blessed are they who contemplate God

Nanak will give his life for them.

The treasury of Your worship is beyond count

Your worshippers worship You in infinite ways;

Worship You who are infinite and without end;

Many are the ways to worship You

Many forms of penance and endless the forms of prayer;

Many a sacred text is read,

Many a way to serve You, including the six karmas;

Says Your slave Nanak, those worshippers are best

Who please the Lord and by Him are blest.

You are the primal Lord, Creator beyond reach

There is none equal to You;

From age to age You are the only one

Forever the only one who gives stability;

What pleases You comes to pass

What You do comes to be;

You created all that exists

You will take it all back as You will;

Your slave Nanak sings Your praises

Who knows all that is worth knowing.

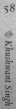

toon karta sachiar mainda saeen

Guru Ram Das

Those who serve the Creator and Master find peace of mind.

You are the true Creator, You are my Master
What pleases You will come to pass,
What You give, I receive.

All that exists belongs to You
You are worshipped for Your creation;
To those You are pleased with,
You grant the jewel of Your name.
Men of God find it, followers of Mammon lose it;
You abandon the worldly, clasp the godly to Your bosom.

You are the mighty river, all within You is contained

Without You nothing exists;

All living creatures are Your playthings

Some get separated from You

Others by Your grace merge in You.

Those You give the gift of wisdom do You appraise

And forever sing songs in Your praise.

He who serves You, finds peace of mind

And in the Lord, he gently a place finds.

You are the Creator, you the Executor

There is none besides you,

You create and keep everything in Your sight.

Says Your slave Nanak, for the godly You came to light.

tit sarvariyai bhaeelay nivaasa

GURU NANAK

We live in a wicked world, our sins take us down the depths of hell.
Our only hope of salvation is prayer in the company of the God-fearing.

A whirlpool of boiling water is our abode
Our feet are clogged with the love of worldly things
We see people sink into those quicksands.

O my stupid heart yet know you not
If you forget the one God
All that is good in you will rot.

I am neither saintly, truthful nor erudite
I was born a fool and foolish I remain
Nanak pleads with You in earnest
Grant me refuge among those who You never forget.

bhaee parapat maanukh dehuriya

GURU ARJAN DEV

In the cycle of births, deaths and rebirths, being born as human is the rare opportunity to mingle with the Lord. Do not waste it in idle pursuits.

You have been granted the human form
Now is the time to meet your Lord Govinda!
No other activity will be of any avail
In the company of the holy, sing praises of the Name.

Prepare yourself to swim across life's fearful ocean
Do not waste life by dabbling in colourful illusions.

We have not earned merit through prayer or penance
Nor exercised control over our minds;
Nor performed sacred duties assigned to us,
Neither have we served men of God;
We are lowly, says Nanak, our acts those of sinners,
We seek refuge in You, so save our honour.

chaupayees

GURU GOBIND SINGH

The 'chaupayees' (quatrains) composed by the warrior Guru, Gobind Singh, were added to Rehras by Sikh scholars after the tenth Guru's demise. The Guru's prayer asking God for help in fighting evil forces is evident in this composition.

Extend Your hand, be my protector
Fulfill my mind's desire;
Your blessed feet be my mind's repose
Cherish me like a relation close.

Of all my foes be the destroyer
Extend me Your hand, be my saviour;
Bless my family with everlasting peace
Creator, preserve my Sikhs and devotees.

Save me with Your own hands I pray
Slay all my enemies today;
Let all my wishes come true
Give me an unending thirst for worshipping You.

Make me meditate on none but You

Whatever I wish, I get from You;

Help my Sikhs and devotees cross life's ocean

Single out my enemies and slay them one by one.

With Your own hands uplift me

From fear of death set me free;

Forever remain on my side

May your sabre and banner by me abide.

Protect me, O Great Protector

Lord of saints, helper of your loved ones;

Always friend of the poor, foe of the evil remain

Lord, the fourteen worlds are within Your domain.

When the right time came You created Brahma the creator

When the right time came You created Shiva the destroyer;

At the right time, You sent Vishnu the preserver

Eternal time is your plaything forever.

When You who made Shiva an ascetic, recluse,

And then Brahma Vedic knowledge pursue;

To that moment, when You adorned the universe

I render my salutation.

He who did the entire world create

Also created gods, demons and yakshas;

He is the alpha and omega of time, the only incarnation

Understand that He is my only Guru.

To Him alone I offer salutation

All subjects are Whose creation;
Who bestowed goodness and virtue on them
And in a trice all enemies overran.

The throbbing of every heart He hears
Pain of the good and wicked He knows;
From the tiny ant to the mighty elephant
He casts a benign look on all and is content.

When the godly suffer, He too suffers
When they are happy, He too rejoices;
The pain of those in pain He shares
The beating of every heart He hears.

In expansive mood the Creator did the world create
His creatures different shapes and forms did take;
Whenever He withdraws in Himself on a whim
All of them will merge in Him.

The world comprises diverse forms and living things
Each praises You according to its understanding;
You Yourself remain aloof from everything
Your mystery is known only to the wise
      and in books of learning.

Formless, immaculate, self-supporting
Primal, stainless, beyond time, self-born;

Only fools try to probe into His existence

Even sacred texts know not His essence.

To mislead people He sculpted a stone

To the great fool the secret remained unknown;

He calls it Mahadev, Shiva eternal

And remains ignorant of the Formless One.

Depending on one's capability

Everyone describes God differently;

Your vast expanse cannot on paper be inscribed

How and when You first made the world cannot be described.

You are in many forms manifest

At one place You are a beggar, at another a king;

You create life from egg, womb and sweat

And from the earth many riches beget.

At some places You are like a flower-bedecked

    king sitting on his throne

At others You are like a hermit shrunken to the bone;

Your creation is a display of wonderment

You were before time, through the ages, self-existent.

Protect me now, to You I pray

Uplift my Sikhs, my enemies slay;

Wherever forces of evil, power wield

Crush the filthy lot in the battlefield.

Those who come under Your flag and hegemony
Their wicked enemies die in terrible agony;
Those who fall at Your feet and seek protection
For all their difficulties You find solutions.

Those who to the timeless God but once do pray
Will never again see an evil day;
At all times He will be their protector
All evil-doers He will instantly scatter.

Those upon whom You look with favour
Their sufferings will at once be over;
In their homes they'll find occult powers,
        wealth and all such
Evil forces will not even their shadows touch.

Those who meditate on Him even once will see
From fear of the noose of death they are free;
A man who invokes Your name
Is freed of misery, evil and pain.

In the battlefield Your protection I crave
Extend Your hand and Your servant save;
In every place You be my helper
From wickedness and sorrow grant me shelter.

swaiya

Guru Gobind Singh

Here the tenth Guru expounds, since he found the 'True' Guru,
all other guides, preachings, doctrines have faded into oblivion,
and he speaks His word.

Ever since I clutched Your feet,

My eyes have not beheld another.

With Ram, Rahim, Puran and Koran and others I did not bother.

Of Smritis, Shastras, Vedas and other texts I took no notice.

It is by virtue of Your banner and Your sword,

What I have written is not mine but Your sacred word.

Khushwant Singh

doehra

Guru Gobind Singh

The Guru declares, he has found his final abode, where he shall live as His slave.

I passed by all doors before I stopped at Yours
Hold me in Your arms, and my honour save
Gobind will forever be Your slave.

anand bhayaa meyree maai

Guru Amar Das

When the seeker finds the Guru he was seeking, he rejoices and bursts out in songs of praise.

Mother, my heart is full of joy

For I have found my True Guru;

I found the True Guru following the gentle path of 'Sahaj'

My heart resounds with cries of felicitation

Jewel-like ragas and their families of fairy-like houris

Have come to sing hymns of praise;

They within whom Hari resides, divine hymns sing

Says Nanak, I have attained bliss because the True Guru I did find.

My heart, ever abide with the Lord Hari

Abide with the Lord and forget all your misery;

Gathering you within Himself

He will sort out all your affairs.

In every way He is your Master

Why then let Him out of your mind?

Says Nanak, my mind forever with the Hari abide.

Master true, what is it that is not in Your house?

There is everything there

Only those You choose to give find it.

Lord, grant me the gift of ever singing Your praise

So Your name gets imprinted on my mind.

The hearts of those wherein dwells the Name

Always resound with hymns of praise

Asks Nanak, True Lord, what is there not found in Your house?

Name of the True Lord is my support

With the True Name's help, I lost all my hungers

It gave me peace of mind, contentment and fulfilled all my desires

Forever may my life be sacrificed to the Guru who is so great

Says Nanak, ye men of God, cherish His words

For the name of the True One is my mainstay.

All five kinds of musical instruments

Play in the hearts of the blessed;

In their blessed homes plays celestial music

Where God has infused His magic and might.

And the five evils (lust, anger, greed, self-love and arrogance)
    are suppressed

And the fear of death is no more

Only those who were predestined

Attach themselves and the True Name find.

Says Nanak, there is always happiness

Where uninterrupted divine music plays.

Hearing the divine music all your heart's desires will be fulfilled.

You will find the great Creator,

All your worldly cares will disappear;

Pain, sickness, worry will vanish

When you hear the true hymns of praise.

Pious and holy men will be overjoyed, assures the True Guru.

Purified are they who hear,

And purified they who sing

The Lord is to be found in His words

Says Nanak, you clasp the sacred feet of the Guru

And you will hear divine music for eternity.

mundavaani

GURU ARJUN

The Guru sums up all that is to be found in evensong.

On this platter you will find three things;

Truth, contentment and contemplation

Also the nectar of the name of the Lord

Which gives sustenance to life

He who imbibes and ingests it will be saved

No one can afford to give it up

Preserve it in your hearts forever and ever.

In the darkness spread over the world,

You will be saved by clasping the feet of the Lord

Says Nanak, for the whole expanse is the Lord's.

tera keeta jato naahin

Guru Arjan Dev

Rehras culminates in thanksgiving to the Lord.
This shloka was originally placed at the end of the first compilation
of the Granth Sahib by Guru Arjan.

All that You have done for me is beyond my comprehension,

I am because of You.

Ignorant, bereft of all virtue,

Still You took mercy on me.

After the mercy, You showered divine grace,

Let me befriend the True Guru

Says Nanak, His name gives me life,

My body and mind shall ever thrive.

acknowledgements

I would like to thank Reema Anand for helping me with the translation of the Rehras.

My thanks, also, to Mohit Suneja and Maithili Doshi Aphale for the beautiful illustrations and design.